CANADA GOOSE POOP OR DUCK POOP?

By Colin Matthews

Gareth Stevens
PUBLISHING

Please visit our website, www.garethstevens.com. For a free color catalog of all our high-quality books, call toll free 1-800-542-2595 or fax 1-877-542-2596.

Library of Congress Cataloging-in-Publication Data

Names: Matthews, Colin, author.
Title: Canada goose poop or duck poop? / Colin Matthews.
Description: New York : Gareth Stevens Publishing, [2020] | Series: The scoop on poop | Includes index.
Identifiers: LCCN 2018019251| ISBN 9781538229521 (library bound) | ISBN 9781538233337 (paperback) | ISBN 9781538233344 (6 pack)
Subjects: LCSH: Canada goose–Juvenile literature. | Ducks–Juvenile literature. | Animal droppings–Juvenile literature.
Classification: LCC QL696.A52 M378 2020 | DDC 598.4/178–dc23
LC record available at https://lccn.loc.gov/2018019251

Published in 2020 by
Gareth Stevens Publishing
111 East 14th Street, Suite 349
New York, NY 10003

Copyright © 2020 Gareth Stevens Publishing

Designer: Sarah Liddell
Editor: Therese Shea

Photo credits: Cover, p. 1 Danae Abreu/Shutterstock.com; p. 5 EEPHOTOGRAPHY/ Shutterstock.com; p. 7 Toronto-Images.Com/Shutterstock.com; p. 9 Bruce MacQueen/ Shutterstock.com; p. 11 Paul Richard Jones/Shutterstock.com; p. 13 nomad-photo.eu/ Shutterstock.com; p. 15 (main) Sandi Cullifer/Shutterstock.com; p. 15 (inset) FotoRequest/ Shutterstock.com; p. 17 Sergey Dzyuba/Shutterstock.com; p. 19 stockphotofan1/ Shutterstock.com.

Printed in the United States of America

CPSIA compliance information: Batch #CS19GS: For further information contact Gareth Stevens, New York, New York at 1-800-542-2595.

CONTENTS

Boldface words appear in the glossary.

Mystery at the Pond

You're going to fish at the pond. You walk to your favorite spot and . . . YUCK! POOP! What animal left it? There are a lot of Canada geese and ducks here. Which was it? Let's learn about each and find out!

Greetings, Canada Goose!

Canada geese have a black head, a black neck, and a light-colored body. They have white "cheeks," too! In the winter, some fly to the southern United States and Mexico. When the weather gets warm, they **migrate** north.

Canada geese usually live in flocks. When **mates** are ready to have a family, they look near water to make a nest. Your pond is perfect for them! Baby geese, or goslings, are ready to fly less than 2 months after **hatching**.

Canada geese live where they find grass, **grain**, and berries to eat. People in many places think geese are pests. A goose can make more than 1 pound (0.5 kg) of poop a day. A flock can make a really big mess!

Dabbling Duck

There are more than 120 duck **species**. True ducks have legs toward the back of their body. They **waddle** on land. True ducks that live near ponds are called dabbling ducks. Mallards are the dabbling ducks that live near your pond.

Female and male mallards look different. Males are colorful, while females have dull-colored feathers. Mallards tip their head into water to find food. They eat shellfish, bugs, and water plants. They find food on land, too.

FEMALE

MALE

15

Female mallards make nests near water. Their ducklings stay near the nest for about 2 months after hatching. Mallards migrate in flocks, just as many Canada geese do. Mallards eat seeds and spread them in their poop. They help plants grow!

Whose Poop?

So, which bird left poop by the pond? Let's look at the **evidence**. Mallard poop is usually greenish with some white on it. It's longer than it is wide. Canada geese poop can be even longer. It's green and white, too!

Now You Know!

There's another piece of evidence to check: footprints! The **stride** of the footprints leading to the poop is almost 1 foot (30 cm) long. A duck's stride is only about 4 inches (10 cm) long. So, the poop was a Canada goose's!

EXAMINE THE EVIDENCE

	CANADA GOOSE	MALLARD
WHERE IT LIVES	NEAR THE POND	NEAR THE POND
WHAT ITS POOP LOOKS LIKE	GREEN AND WHITE	GREEN AND WHITE
LENGTH OF STRIDE	1 FOOT (30 CM)	4 INCHES (10 CM)

IT WAS THE GOOSE'S POOP!

GLOSSARY

evidence: something that helps show or disprove the truth of something

grain: the seeds of plants that are used for food

hatch: to come out of an egg

mate: one of two animals that come together to produce babies

migrate: to move to warmer or colder places for a season

species: a group of animals that are all of the same kind

stride: a long step

waddle: to walk with short steps while moving from side to side

FOR MORE INFORMATION

BOOKS

Borgert-Spaniol, Megan. *Canada Geese*. Minneapolis, MN: Bellwether Media, 2017.

Dicker, Katie. *Duck*. Mankato, MN: Smart Apple Media, 2014.

WEBSITES

Canada Goose
kids.nationalgeographic.com/animals/canada-goose/ #canada-goose-flock-flying.jpg
Check out some facts about Canada geese.

Mallard Duck
kids.nationalgeographic.com/animals/mallard-duck/ #mallard-male-swimming.jpg
How fast can a mallard fly? Find out here!

INDEX